From Alan—

A Touch of His Peace

Other Books in This Series

A Touch of His Peace

MEDITATIONS ON EXPERIENCING THE PEACE
OF GOD WITH ORIGINAL PHOTOGRAPHS BY

CHARLES STANLEY

ZondervanPublishingHouse
Grand Rapids, Michigan

Divisions of HarperCollins*Publishers*

A Touch of His Peace
Copyright © 1993 by Charles F. Stanley
All rights reserved

Requests for information should be addressed to:
Zondervan Publishing House
Grand Rapids, Michigan 49530

Library of Congress Cataloging-in-Publication Data

Stanley, Charles F.
    A touch of his peace : meditations on experiencing the peace of
    God / Charles Stanley.
        p.   cm.
    ISBN 0-310-54550-1 (hard cover)
    1. Peace of mind—Religious aspects—Christianity—Meditations.
    I. Title.
    BV4908.5.S74   1993
    242—dc20   92-43289
                                                                CIP

Edited by Gerard Terpstra
Cover design, interior design, and line illustrations by Art Jacobs

93 94 95 96 97 98 / ❖ MV / 10 9 8 7 6 5 4 3 2 1

This edition is printed on acid-free paper and meets the American National
Standards Institute Z39.48 standard.

Contents

Photographs

Introduction

One of the most comforting passages of Scripture is Jesus' discourse with his disciples in John 13–17. Jesus intimately shares his impending betrayal, arrest, death, and ascension to the Father.

The disciples are worried, puzzled, perplexed. What will they do when Jesus is gone?

In their distress, Jesus speaks these soothing words: "Peace I leave with you; my peace I give you. I do not give to you as the world gives. Do not let your hearts be troubled and do not be afraid" (John 14:27).

Jesus' words of comfort are for us today as well. In our hour of pain, confusion, or fear, we can experience a supernatural peace that steadies and sustains our fretful spirit. Innermost peace is given only by God. While others promise peace, Jesus himself is our peace who lives in us.

Our circumstances may seem intolerable. Our challenges may appear insurmountable. Our obstacles may breed constant, unremitting worry and turmoil. Yet in the midst of our conflicts, Jesus gives us his perfect peace if we will but receive it. It is his to give; and he has chosen to freely extend it to you.

Jesus stills a distraught heart. He calms an anxious mind. He gives rest to the weary and brings blessed refreshment, renewal, and contentment. The God of peace is with you and for you. He is at home in your heart through the presence of the Comforter, the Holy Spirit.

You can consistently experience Christ's peace in every circumstance. He will never leave or forsake you. He will never leave you helpless or hopeless.

It is my prayer that these devotionals will bring a touch of his peace to your life. God does not always take away trouble, but he can and does heal a troubled heart. His peace "transcends all understanding" (Phil. 4:7).

A Touch of His Peace

But now in Christ Jesus you who once were far away have been brought near through the blood of Christ. For he himself is our peace.

Ephesians 2:13–14

Peace with God

The earthquake that shook San Francisco in 1989 did considerable damage to bridges and highways. However, residential destruction was limited primarily to an area along the bay. The ruin was not due to poor construction or proximity to the epicenter of the quake. It occurred because the homes were constructed on land reclaimed from the bay: when the quake struck, the precarious foundation gave way.

In order for peace to endure, it must have an authentic foundation. Our remedies for global, relational, and personal peace are too often built on faulty premises, relying on flawed practices and people to achieve and maintain it.

This was the case for the rebellious people of Jeremiah's day. Mired in greed, guile, and corruption, the priests and prophets promised an artificially contrived peace: "They dress the wound of my people as though it were not serious. 'Peace, peace,' they say, when there is no peace" (Jer. 6:14).

The superficial prescriptions for peace in a world of turmoil will not work apart from a spiritual cornerstone. There is no peace for the wicked, unbelieving person, because God's wrath opposes him. He walks under the sentence of eternal death and burdensome guilt. God and the unrepentant are foes, not friends; and though there may be moments or seasons of peace, the enmity and judgment of God hang over the head and heart of those who do not believe. They are at war with God and strangers to real peace. Death holds nothing but grim punishment and agony for them for eternity.

God has laid the solid foundation for true peace through the Cross of his Son, Jesus Christ. On the tree Jesus shouldered the full fury of the holy God against sin and paved the way through his death for everlasting peace with the Father. The instant you place your trust in Christ for the forgiveness of sin,

you are reconciled to God. The rebellion is over. The conflict has ended. You have been reconciled to God who has made "peace through his blood, shed on the cross" (Col. 1:20).

Because you now have peace *with* God, you can experience the fathomless peace *of* God. You cannot reverse the order. As long as one is God's enemy, enduring peace is unattainable. But once a person looks to the Cross and receives its merits by faith, the peace of God is forever his.

When Christ returns to establish his kingdom on earth, peace will reign universally. Until then, the Christian has the awesome privilege of experiencing and extending the peace of Christ. Still more, he has entered into a personal relationship with Christ marked by a supernatural peace the world cannot duplicate. The right foundation has been laid. Whatever shakes your life may temporarily unsettle you, but it can never disturb your everlasting relationship with the Prince of Peace.

Heavenly Father, I realize that sin has created strife and enmity between you and me. I thank you that Christ's death on the cross satisfied your holy wrath and reconciled me to yourself. Thank you for taking this initiative, Father. I never could have settled the conflict in my own knowledge. You have given me peace that is sure, everlasting, and unfading. You are for me, not against me, and that is cause for unceasing praise and thanksgiving.

TOUCHSTONE

No God, no peace.
Know God, know peace.

Find rest, O my soul, in God alone; my hope comes from him.
Psalm 62:5

Rest for the Weary

The Bible is a book of paradoxes. If we want to live, we must die to self. If we want to achieve greatness, we must humble ourselves and become servants. If we desire to receive, we must first give.

Perhaps one of the strangest paradoxes is found in the book of Hebrews. The author tells the enticing news about entering what he calls a "Sabbath-rest for the people of God" (Heb. 4:9). Just as God rested from his work of creation, so there exists a spiritual state of rest and refreshment for the weary and parched soul of the believer.

What wonderful news! The struggle does not have to be unending. The burden can be laid down. The walk of faith does not have to wear out our souls. But exactly how do we experience this profound rest? Here again is the paradox: "Let us, therefore, make every effort to enter that rest" (Heb. 4:11).

Rest is experienced through diligent effort and vigilance. It seems contradictory, doesn't it? It is the last thing the worn spiritual pilgrim wants to hear. He is at the end of his rope; how is it possible for him to work harder to find divine restoration?

The writer of Hebrews is not at odds with himself, nor is he in conflict with the biblical principle of rest. Rather, he is prescribing the exact remedy for enjoying the abundant Christian life in an entirely new dimension.

Here is the key: "For anyone who enters God's rest also rests from his own work, just as God did from his" (Heb. 4:10).

You are to rest from trying to make yourself acceptable to God. You are as righteous and acceptable in God's eyes today as you will be when you enter his very presence in heaven. God treats you today and forever according to the merits and mediation of the Cross, not your behavior. You are already pleasing to

God. You are already holy and blameless in his eyes. Your actions may not always measure up to your identity, but you are a child of God forever. You can cease from any works of self-righteousness.

We are to rest also from working in the energy of the flesh and live in the energy of the Holy Spirit. Living and working in the strength and power of your talents and abilities will only take you so far. It is a long, uphill climb that leads to eventual exhaustion and burnout.

But living according to the Spirit will bring you into the green pastures and beside the still waters of the Good Shepherd. "For it is God who works in you to will and to act according to his good purpose" (Phil. 2:13). That takes the strain off, doesn't it? That infuses the very power of God into your every thought, word, and deed. God is responsible for you. He saved you. He will sanctify you. He began a good work in you. He will complete it. Surely you are to obey, but you have the power of God to accomplish all that he has planned for your life. Forget manipulation. Reject clever plans. Cease from your own futile efforts to imitate Christ. Enter the rest of God by placing your trust in the finished work of the Cross. Commit your way to him. This is the way of success, endurance, and cherished rest for your innermost being. It is the rest of confident faith in the faithfulness of God.

O Lord, I see that I cannot enter into your peace and rest apart from abandoning all works of self-righteousness. I thank you that I do not have to make myself acceptable to you, for you have already made me acceptable. I gladly yield to the life of the Spirit, allowing him to flow through me. I have come to abide in Christ now, so that his inexhaustible strength may saturate me and flow through me.

TOUCHSTONE

When we come to the end
of ourselves, we are ready
to enter God's rest.

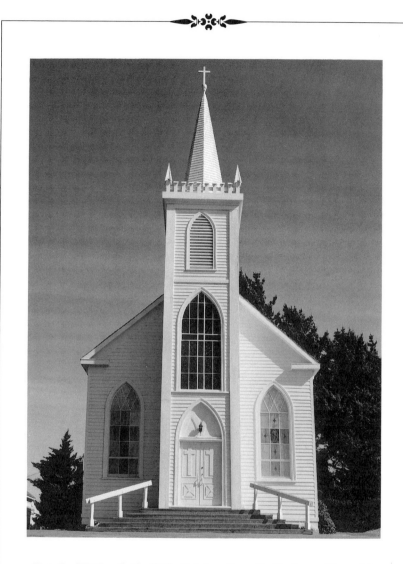

But the [Helper], the Holy Spirit, whom the Father will send in my name, will teach you all things.

John 14:26

The Helper

Jesus was the ultimate realist. Although he spoke often of the abundant life and the blessings of obedience, he never soft-pedaled the opposition, affliction, and suffering each believer would encounter.

Shortly before his death, he reminded his disciples of the rough road ahead of them. He knew the obstacles they would face as they spread the good news of salvation: "I have told you these things, so that in me you may have peace. In this world you will have trouble. But take heart! I have overcome the world" (John 16:33).

When you became a Christian, you began an exciting relationship with Christ; but it did not mean the end of your problems. More than likely, you have discovered intense struggles with temptations, tests, and trials that are an inevitable part of the Christian's road to maturity.

But you can "take heart," for you do have supernatural help in your spiritual journey. Jesus' words of warning were couched in the promise that he would send the Holy Spirit to aid the believer.

Jesus gives you his prevailing peace by giving you his all-sufficient Spirit. The power and person of the Spirit of God indwell you unceasingly. Whatever difficulties you face, the Holy Spirit is ever present to extend the peace of God to your heart and mind.

The Spirit of God will teach you in your perplexity. He is the author of the Scriptures and makes your soul susceptible to the calming reality of God's truth. He will teach you all you need to know, granting wisdom and knowledge for successful living. On many occasions, the Holy Spirit has revealed to me the right solutions to problems that I could not solve in my own strength.

The Spirit of God will guide you in your confusion. You do not know what lies ahead. In fact, you don't know what will happen in the very next minute. But the Holy Spirit does. He can guide you unerringly in his ways if you are willing to wait on him and accept his counsel.

The Spirit of God will comfort you in your heartache. Grief and loss are part of the human existence. The Holy Spirit tenderly sustains and upholds you in such seasons. The Greek word for the designation of the Holy Spirit as Counselor is *parakletos*, that is, "one called alongside to help and aid." What a marvelous description of the One whom God gives to us to experience his transcendent peace.

Jesus overcame the world by triumphing over every temptation, defeating the devil, and becoming obedient even to the point of death. This same Jesus lives in you today through the Holy Spirit who extends the precious peace of God to you at every turn. The Holy Spirit is God's gift of peace to you.

Lord, I do admit that at times I feel devoid of your peace. But it is not so, because your Spirit lives in me. Teach me to depend on you for your help. Make me aware of the Spirit's constant presence. Thank you, Holy Spirit, that you are willing to give me God's peace in any circumstance. I receive it gratefully. Sustain me with your peace.

TOUCHSTONE

*The Helper is with you,
for you, and in you.*

Without warning, a furious storm came up on the lake, so that the waves swept over the boat.

Matthew 8:24

When
the Storms Come

Inever paid much attention to hurricane reports until I pastored a church in Florida. Each fall the watch began for climatic disturbances that could eventually result in a full-scale hurricane with surging tides and destructive winds.

A hurricane did not strike my home; but I did learn a lot about them, including the mysterious "eye of the storm," an uncanny center of calm in the midst of fury.

The disciples once found themselves in a violent storm on the Sea of Galilee. The waves washed into the boat, the winds wailed, and the disciples feared for their lives. A weary and sleeping Jesus was awakened by his panic-stricken followers. He then demonstrated his deity by rebuking the turbulent winds and turning chaos into calm.

You may be in such a storm. It could be emotional, financial, or physical. It may be in your marriage or in your job. Like the disciples, you may be afraid and wonder where God is.

Know this: As there is calm in the eye of the storm, so there can be calm in the midst of your problem, because Jesus is at the center of your life. He is not asleep. He is not immune to your pain, for he himself has suffered the deep pain of the human lot.

He is on board with you and capable of demonstrating his magnificent deity to you in a myriad of ways. This is the truth that brings peace to your soul and calm to your emotions. This is the anchor that holds you in place when everything else seems to pull you loose from your moorings.

You are hand in hand with him in the storm, and you have his presence at the core of your life. There he can bring his peace even if the gale of adversity continues to assault you relentlessly.

The apostle Paul wrote that the mystery of the gospel that has been made known is "Christ in you, the hope of glory" (Col. 1:27). Christ may calm the storm by removing the problem, or he will calm you as you go through the tempest. He is at the center of your life to reveal himself in new and majestic ways so that you may worship him and thank him.

Jesus is Immanuel—God with us. Though he may seem silent at times, he is never still. Though he may seem absent, he is always present. Though he may seem uncaring, he is positioning you for his greatest blessing.

Jesus is in the storm with you and capable of doing the impossible. That is your "hope of glory" and the cornerstone of peace for any storm.

Lord, I am caught off guard sometimes by unexpected problems. I find peace so elusive. I cannot get my mind off my problems. Help me to turn to you and know that you can quiet my storms with promises from your Word, with an assuring touch of your Spirit. I am so grateful you are with me in the storms.

TOUCHSTONE

*Whatever is at the center
of your life determines
your course.*

When Peter came to Antioch, I opposed him to his face, because he was clearly in the wrong.

Galatians 2:11

Caring Enough to Confront

The way of peace is not always the path of least resistance. On occasion, the means of establishing peace is confrontation. It is not a popular choice, and it certainly should not be the standard one. However, when a problem between people reaches the boiling point or when you witness continued injustice and inequity in a particular circumstance, confrontation may be the solution.

Paul was forced to choose that option to deal with Peter's hypocrisy. The acknowledged leader of the disciples, Peter was afraid of Jewish opinion regarding his relationship with the Gentiles. He timidly appeased the Jewish Christians by withdrawing from Gentile fellowship upon Paul's visit. His errant behavior was drawing Jewish believers into legalism, and Paul bluntly rebuked him.

When confrontation is necessary, it must be accomplished in a biblical framework and for biblical purposes. Your motivation must be pure. That means you must spend considerable time in prayer, asking God to cleanse you from selfish considerations. God is concerned with the heart; and if confrontation serves only to vent your anger, then you are not approaching the problem God's way.

Confrontation should be reserved for situations that involve a clear violation of biblical principle or spiritual standard of conduct. There will always be people of different temperaments who annoy us or circumstances that irritate us. These are best accepted as God's chisels for conforming us to his image: "A man's wisdom gives him patience; it is to his glory to overlook an offense" (Prov. 19:11).

The goal of confrontation should be correction, not condemnation. As God's ambassadors, we are called to reconcile, helping to heal and mend broken relationships. If we confront someone whose behavior is plainly and consistently wrong, our objective should be to guide him to the truth that sets him free, not to vindicate ourselves. We must do all of this in the context of gentleness and kindness, realizing that this is the way God deals with us in our disobedience.

Keep your confrontation on the personal and private level. Do it as Paul did, "face to face." Keep it strictly between you and the offending person. Don't unwisely share the problem with friends in an attempt to find support. If confrontation succeeds in solving the problem, peace will supplant the reign of tension. If it doesn't succeed, leave the matter with God and the results in his capable hands.

I do not like confrontation, Lord; and when I do think about a need to confront, I usually get angry. Give me the courage I need to confront the problem your way, always remembering the undeserved love you shower on me despite my erratic behavior. I ask for your wisdom to help me know when to confront someone and when to remain silent. Thank you that your goal is peace and that I can count on your guidance.

TOUCHSTONE

*Confrontation sometimes is
God's hard road to a
peaceful destination.*

He has given us new birth into a living hope through the resurrection of Jesus Christ from the dead, and into an inheritance that can never perish, spoil, or fade—kept in heaven for you.
1 Peter 1:3–4

Saved and Sure

I have counseled people in many distressing situations, but I cannot think of any worse predicament than that of the people who are unsure of their eternal security. For such, the Christian life is an unsteady tightrope, precariously walked by good works. Any stumble, and their eternal destiny is in doubt.

I cannot think of anything that causes more misery. Such people have no semblance of peace, only intense agony over whether or not they have lived up to God's standard. They have only a hope of heaven, no guarantee.

This kind of living is treacherous and, when examined, is shown to be wholly derived from false teaching and erroneous thinking. If your eternal security is directly coupled with your good works, then how good must you be? How good is good enough? How do you know whether you have passed the test or not? What happens if you die on a bad day?

Can you see the fallacy and confusion this kind of theology breeds? Yet multitudes—and that is probably an underestimation—are caught in its bewildering web. All one needs is a heart open to the truth of Scripture and the power of the Cross to be set free and know peace in an entirely new dimension.

God's standard is perfection. Now, how do you live up to that? It is impossible; and that is precisely why God sent his perfect Son to be our substitutionary, all-sufficient atoning sacrifice at Calvary. Christianity is a liberating faith; and Jesus Christ is our Deliverer, bearing our sin along with its penalty—death—and providing full forgiveness of our sin by faith in his person and work.

You are saved by grace through faith in Christ and kept for all eternity by grace through faith in Christ. Good works do matter for the Christian, but for the purpose of rewards in heaven, not as a means to escape judgment. Once you believe, you can never be condemned again, never judged again for your sins. Jesus was condemned and judged on Calvary by God, once and for all.

You can know the peace that eternal security in Christ brings as you accept the truth that you are saved and kept by Christ's performance, not yours. You cannot fall from grace, because salvation is but an introduction into a life of grace that never ends (Rom. 5:1–2). Your eternal security has been won and is preserved by Jesus Christ, not your works. Once you are saved, nothing can loosen God's eternal grip on you. You are forever forgiven and assured of heaven because Jesus now lives in you; his Spirit is the down payment for what is to come.

Your eternal security is rooted in Christ. He saved you. He keeps you. He has prepared a place for you in heaven. You have a firm reservation that no sin can cancel. Accept this truth and exchange the misery of self-righteousness for the joy of being in the righteousness of God in Christ. You are eternally secure in Christ.

Father, how liberating it is to know that my eternal security is in your hands, not mine. Once a saint, I am always a saint. Nothing can change that, and nothing can take away my home in heaven. It is Christ's work of forgiveness and indwelling life that makes my eternal security firm. Thank you for the remarkable peace this truth brings.

TOUCHSTONE

You can never fall from grace when it is God who keeps you.

God is our refuge and strength, an ever-present help in trouble.
Psalm 46:1

The Hiding Place

You have a refuge, a stronghold, a fortress to which you may come for stability and calm when life's pressures mount and your inner peace quivers. During his wilderness exile the psalmist David used this vivid imagery more than any other Scripture writer. God, not the numerous caves and caverns of the desert mountains, was his true shelter. Jehovah God kept him, protected him, and sustained him physically, spiritually, and emotionally.

Christ is the believer's refuge, the Person to whom we may come with every complaint and dilemma. The Old Testament speaks of dwelling in the "shelter of his wings" (Ps. 61:4), referring to the nearness and protection of the heavenly Father in times of trouble. Can anything or anyone really permanently harm us when God is our shield? If Jesus is the defense of our life, we will not cower before people or circumstances. If God is for us, who can be against us?

How do we make Christ our refuge? How do we come to that place of knowing that he is responsible for our safekeeping? The writer of Proverbs gives us one clue: "The name of the LORD is a strong tower; the righteous run to it and are safe" (Prov. 18:10).

He is El Shaddai, the Almighty God. This name literally means the All-Sufficient One or the All-Bountiful One. He fulfills every promise of Scripture and is faithful to perform his Word. He is El Elyon, the Most High God, who rules over people and nations and whose strength and power no one can resist. He is your impenetrable shield and your protector. He is El Olam, the Everlasting One, the God who is eternally consistent. He is the stability of your life when things seem to unravel. He is El Roi, the God who sees. He watches over you, seeing and knowing all that happens, and he comes to your aid.

He is Jehovah Jireh, the God who provides all your needs according to his unlimited bounty.

The names of God, and there are many, tell us who he is and how he acts. They are the reflection of his attributes and character—his love, grace, mercy, kindness, goodness, faithfulness, gentleness. This is the God to whom you may run for refuge, to whom you may go for shelter and help. The problems may not subside; but when you make God your hiding place, you may confidently face the day secure in his provision, help, and protection.

God is our refuge also as we come to him in heartfelt honesty with our needs: "Trust in him at all times, O people; pour out your hearts to him, for God is our refuge" (Ps. 62:8). Turning to Christ and releasing our fears and anxieties in earnest prayer is a powerful step into the refuge of the everlasting arms.

Lord, I want to know you better so that I may trust you more. You really are my refuge and stronghold. Teach me to run to you quickly so that I may find shelter in your everlasting arms. There I know I am safe.

TOUCHSTONE

The shadow of the Almighty
is large enough to
encompass every need.

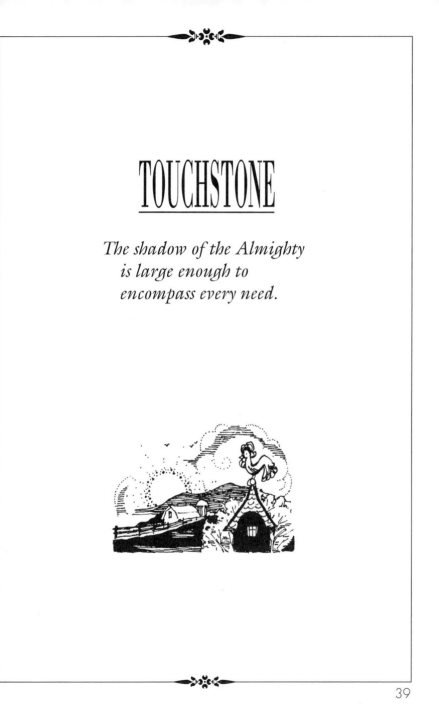

The grass withers and the flowers fall, but the word of our God stands forever.

Isaiah 40:8

Passing Feelings

Picture this scene in your mind: You are out on a boat in the middle of a placid lake. It's fall, and the leaves are a crayon box full of colors. Canadian geese fly overhead. After slowly rowing on the lake for an hour, you return to the dock that is connected to a cabin on the shore. You sip a mug of hot chocolate and sit on the porch rocker as the sun fades.

Now imagine this scene: You are stuck in the middle of bumper-to-bumper traffic on the interstate. You are already late for work. Sirens scream as they rush by on the shoulder to reach the wreck a few hundred feet in front of you. Impatient drivers surround you. Your cup of hot coffee spills on your lap as you hit the brakes to avoid rear-ending the car in front of you.

If you recorded your emotional response in these instances, your feelings would differ widely. The first setting evokes feelings of serenity, whereas the second ignites flashes of anger and irritability.

Feelings rush in and out. They rise and fall with circumstances and are invariably hinged to the thermometer of our emotions. We know what it is like to be flushed with anger one hour and smiling the next. Emotions are part of our personality and are God-given, but they were not bestowed on us as reliable spiritual gauges. Housed in a body of sin and subject to a variety of external influences, they are false props for the genuine peace of God.

God's peace is anchored to his Word, not our feelings. The unchanging revelation of Scripture is our accurate and predictable guide for authentic, godly peace. God's Word is eternal fact, everlasting truth that can be counted on regardless of our emotions.

We may feel hopeless. God's Word says our hope is sure and certain and can never be taken away. We may feel power-

less, but God's Word says we have all the strength we need in him. We may feel lonely, but God's Word says he is always with us. We may feel we cannot approach God, but his Word says we have free access to him through his Son, Jesus Christ.

Decide now that you will not let your feelings dictate your awareness and experience of God's peace. Lean your whole weight upon the truth of God's Word and refuse to be shaken. Only in this way can darkness become light, doubt become faith, and despair become confident hope. Don't suppress your emotions, but let them lead you to the Rock of God's truth. That is what standing on the Word is all about. God will not let you fall.

I realize my feelings are not totally reliable gauges for experiencing your peace, Lord. How thankful I am that you never change and that you steady me with your peace as I learn to depend on your truth. I submit my emotions to you and ask you to keep them under the reign of your abiding peace.

TOUCHSTONE

*The peace of God is hinged
on his Word, not on my
emotions.*

And my God will meet all your needs according to his glorious riches in Christ Jesus.

Philippians 4:19

Unmet Needs

A well-known Christian author and thinker once said,
"Mankind is one vast need." What an apt description of the
human lot. As long as our needs—emotional, spiritual, physical,
material—are being met, we are relatively happy. But when one
or more of our needs is unfilled, peace is a scarce commodity.

Learning to deal with such unmet needs while maintaining
a positive faith is a critical step in experiencing the kind of contentment that Christ promises us for every circumstance. That
learning process begins by realizing that Jesus understands our
needs and has the power to meet them. In his humanity, Christ
participated in the full scope of human existence, including
needs. He was hungry. He was thirsty. He needed rest. He
endured agony of soul before his death. And now, having suffered all of that, he feels for us. He hurts for us. He knows our
needs.

"But if God knows my needs and can meet them, why
hasn't he?" As a pastor, I have heard that question many times
from singles who yearn to be married, from the unemployed
who only want a decent job, from wives who long for their hus-
bands to tenderly communicate love to them.

In a way, all of these are expressions of man's three basic
needs—a sense of belonging, a sense of competence, and a
sense of worth. These are the deepest emotional and spiritual
needs of the soul; and when they are unmet, they create the
most intense pain.

Yet, if we have a genuine need (as distinguished from an
illegitimate desire) that is not met, we must look at several
things. Have we been willfully disobedient to God in some
area? Are we refusing to wait on God to meet our needs in his
way and in his time? Are we wrongfully manipulating people or
circumstances? Is our motivation misdirected? Is God trying to

teach us something? Is God calling us to repentance or leading us to trust him in a greater way?

During the delay—the time between when you have asked God to meet a need and the time he supplies that need—you must refuse every false means of satisfying your need. There will be the temptation to seek to meet your needs in your way, in your timing. Yielding to temptation may superficially and temporarily meet your need, but it will not last. The consequences will create only more frustration.

The only Person who can satisfy all your needs is Jesus Christ. Because of the Cross, where you were reconciled to God, you are of great value to him, you belong to him, and you are accepted by him. An intimate relationship with Jesus Christ is really the only enduring means to meet all of your needs. You can never exhaust the reservoir of his grace, mercy, and love for you.

God will meet your needs according to his good will. It may take time. The means and end may not be what you anticipated. But if you will seek to find your deepest needs met through your friendship with Christ, you will truly discover that God does indeed supply every need according to his superabundant riches. Jesus never fails.

How often I have looked to someone or something else to meet my needs, Lord. I realize this is tempting but futile. Help me to accept the truth that you are the only One who can truly satisfy my innermost longings. I turn to you now and ask that you will meet my needs in your way. I know that you only want my best, so I submit all to you.

TOUCHSTONE

When you have Christ, you have everything you need.

*You will keep in perfect peace him whose mind is steadfast,
because he trusts in you.*

Isaiah 26:3

The Right Focus

A large portrait of Daniel in the lion's den hangs prominently in my study. There is a story behind that painting that God used to indelibly imprint a crucial biblical truth in my heart—a truth that has kept me on the course of faith through many years and numerous trials.

Several years ago an elderly member of our congregation asked me to visit her. We chatted for a while before she drew my attention to the painting of Daniel on her apartment wall. She knew I was enduring some particularly stressful circumstances at the time, and she gave some godly counsel I will never forget.

"Tell me what you see in the painting," she quizzed.

I responded in a matter-of-fact manner. "Well, I see some lions, a few shafts of light, and Daniel."

"There is something else I think you should notice," she continued, obviously aware I had not gotten the message. "Take a closer look at Daniel and you will see that his eyes are not on the lions but on God."

The Holy Spirit instantly gripped me with a spiritual principle that has sustained me in many adversities: When I choose to put my eyes on the Lord, not my situation, God will take me through the problem.

"Looking to Jesus" is not a spiritual cliché. It is a bedrock act of faith anchored to the Scriptures and a spiritual exercise that can mean the difference between victory and defeat in our personal spiritual lives. It is a matter of focus and choice. I can decide whether I will be obsessed with my problems, constantly churning them up in my mind and spirit, or deliberately concentrate on the Lord Jesus Christ, who can help me solve my problems. Dwelling on my circumstances generates anxiety, stress, anger, and fear. It drains me of spiritual vitality and saps

my faith. But choosing to fix my mind on Christ—on his presence and power—builds my faith and provides the right atmosphere for true peace to prevail.

The Greek word the writer of Hebrews used for "fix" literally means to "look away from all else that distracts." I have plenty of distractions each day and so do you. The way to peace is focusing on Christ, feeding on a regular diet of his Word, setting our will to obey his Word, and thanking him that he will fulfill his promises to us.

Are you so overwhelmed that you have lost sight of Jesus? Daniel kept his eyes on heaven, and his troubles on earth were dealt with by the mighty power of God. Fix your gaze on the certainty of God's supernatural help and love, and your problems will be put into perspective. The lion's roar will be stilled.

Father, I am quickly and easily distracted by daily demands. I have so much to do and think about that I lose sight of your presence and goodness. Right now, I choose by faith to look to you for help and guidance. And I trust you for the outcome. Thank you for the peace that you give me as I fix my eyes on you and see the light of your countenance.

TOUCHSTONE

*Fix your eyes on Christ, and
your problem will be put
into perspective.*

Now I want you to know, brothers, that what has happened to me has really served to advance the gospel.

Philippians 1:12

Through the Forest

I love the wilderness. I thoroughly enjoy fishing and hunting and the abundant opportunities for scenic photography. The serene surroundings give me plenty of time to contemplate on the greatness and goodness of God. Often the only means by which I can reach many areas is by traversing roughly cut logging roads. The journey is arduous; but the destination is worth the discomfort.

Similarly, hardship is frequently the road we must travel to experience personal peace. That may appear illogical on the surface; but the Bible is filled with examples of men and women facing dire circumstances that paradoxically served to promote, not destroy, God's peace.

The book of Philippians, authored by Paul, is one of the most encouraging epistles in the New Testament. It is upbeat, rings with joy, and has much to say about the peace of God. What is unusual is that Philippians (as well as several of Paul's other letters) was penned from inside a Roman prison, where chains were part of his daily wardrobe. That's not the setting you or I would have in mind for such a joyous epistle, but Paul understood a life-changing principle that can make peace possible in any environment.

He knew that every occasion was an opportunity to "advance the gospel." He seized on a word picture that portrays woodcutters hacking and clearing a trail through forests and hills for armies to tread. Rather than becoming discouraged and faint-hearted, Paul actually saw his problems as divine woodcutters, making a way for the gospel to spread. Is this how you view your obstacles? Can you say with Paul that your circumstances are helping pave the way for Christ to live through you and make himself known to others in the process? You may have some chains of your own—emotional hurts, physical afflictions, relational yokes—but God can turn them into sharp sickles that make a path for spiritual growth and advancement. You are never chained to your circumstances as long as you keep in mind they are tools for genuine spiritual maturity.

The circumstances and people you deal with today are blazing a trail for the gospel of Christ to become real in your life and a solid testimony to others. It is a rough road, but the view later on can be spectacular.

Thank you, Lord, for the many chances to advance the good news in my life and in the lives of others. I would not choose such sharp tools as you do, but I realize this often is the only way for me to grow and experience your peace. Help me to keep my mind on the result and what is being accomplished as I go through rough times. These difficulties are for my good. They will enhance my communion with you. They will bring about positive results. Never let me lose sight of this truth.

TOUCHSTONE

*My circumstances are
opportunities to advance
the gospel.*

You intended to harm me, but God intended it for good to
accomplish what is now being done, the saving of many lives.
Genesis 50:20

Who's in Charge?

A sudden financial crisis can wipe away our carefully constructed budget. A completely unexpected illness can idle us for months. Unplanned delays can quickly obliterate our carefully crafted schedules.

These scenarios and a multitude of other story lines can leave us with one feeling that can intimidate us more than any other—the feeling that things are out of control. We are usually comfortable with our ability to handle diverse situations. But incidents occur that are beyond the reach of our competence and capability. They shake us to the core. What can we do? How do we handle something that we literally have no control over? How do we experience God's peace in such wildly frightening settings?

There is only one prescription for peace in such times— absolute faith in the sovereignty and providence of God. The providence of God has been defined by J. I. Packer as "the unceasing activity of the Creator whereby, in overflowing bounty and goodwill, he upholds his creatures in ordered existence, guides and governs all events, circumstances, and free acts of angels and men, and directs everything to its appointed goal, for his own glory." That is not mere theological fluff. That is solid truth you can rely on when your personal world is rocked with calamity, uncertainty, or adversity of any form.

God is in control when all appears out of control. He is able to work good out of evil and to take disastrous events and turn them around for your welfare. As chaotic and happenstance as some things seem, God is actively working out his benevolent, providential plan for your life. Nothing can thwart his purpose for you. Nothing can shake him.

When you know that God is in control, you can face change—unexpected or anticipated—with confidence. All is

held together by his omnipotent hand. All is within his loving care. He is not surprised or frustrated or foiled by anything or anyone. Through God's sovereignty Joseph could see the good hand of God behind his years of enslavement and imprisonment working perpetually to eventually bless him and all of Egypt (Gen. 50:20).

When you know God is in control, you can give thanks in everything, knowing he is arranging all things by his providential care for your personal welfare. It is impossible to be grateful in tough times if you are not resting in the sovereignty of God. When you acknowledge the providence of God, his peace will keep you and guard you. It will steady your soul with the good news that God is in complete control of your circumstances and is working toward his appointed end, which will ultimately benefit you and others.

Thank you that you are a sovereign God. I am not a victim of chance or circumstance but a chosen child of God who belongs to the almighty heavenly Father with whom there is no change. I believe that you are in charge of every area of my life. You are not the author of evil. Evil is only an instrument in your good hand, and nothing can happen to me outside of your permissive will. Thank you for the settling peace this truth brings to me.

TOUCHSTONE

*There is absolutely nothing
that will happen to you
today that your loving
Father doesn't already
know about.*

Grace and peace to you from God our Father and the Lord Jesus Christ.

Galatians 1:3

Grace and Peace

Grace and peace are twin sisters, grace being the firstborn. Where grace abounds, peace thrives. Where grace is stunted, peace shrivels. The salutation of every New Testament letter penned by the apostle Paul contains the hearty greeting "Grace and peace."

If you do not understand grace, you can never understand Christianity. It is a religion of grace. The Bible is the good news of God's grace in Christ Jesus. We begin by grace at salvation and continue by grace each day. We can never earn God's acceptance; we can receive the gift of salvation only through faith in Christ. Once saved, we cannot secure God's approval through good works but only receive the grace of his Spirit to help us accomplish his will.

Grace excludes all human boasting—it boasts only in Christ. It is the perpetual, undeserved goodness and kindness of God that can never be turned away by anything the believer does, says, or thinks. It is the unbroken circle of God's astounding lovingkindness. There is no need to strive for God's love; you already have it through the grace of the Cross. You stand and walk on the same level ground of grace each day.

Think of grace this way: Grace is whatever you may need, whenever you need it. Do you need strength? Grace begets strength. Do you need wisdom? Grace bestows insight. Do you need peace? Grace stills the waters. Do you need comfort? Grace soothes the soul and spirit.

But grace does more than this. Because the fountainhead is God himself, grace gives and gives and gives. The grace of God is not just barely enough to scrape by with. It exceeds and surpasses our most pressing demands. Grace carries you from strength to strength. It gives wisdom liberally. It grants peace that never wanes. It brings comfort that heals and sustains.

You live in the sunshine of God's unconditional grace. You can draw on his inexhaustible, immeasurable, unsearchable reservoir of grace forever and never diminish its fullness. You are no longer under the law, which says "do" and breeds defeat and discouragement, but under grace, which says "done" in Christ and brings triumph and courage.

Paul told Timothy to be "strong in the grace that is in Christ Jesus" (2 Tim. 2:1). When you are "strong in grace," you can stand in any turbulence, face any foe, and deal with any disturbance in the riches of God's complete sufficiency. You are free also to extend grace to others, regardless of their behavior. You swim in the sea of God's grace that buoys you in times of trouble and quenches every thirst. Grace is more than amazing. It's awesome, and it is custom-designed for your every need.

How much I need your grace, O Lord. How quickly I turn to other cisterns of help, all broken and shallow. But when I call on the God of all grace, I receive all I need. I am never disappointed, never short-changed. Thank you for saving me by your grace and keeping me by your grace.

TOUCHSTONE

Be strong in grace, and
peace will be your
constant companion.

For from him and through him and to him are all things.
Romans 11:36

The Big Picture

More often than not, it is the little irritations in life that fracture my peace. I usually handle the crises capably, but the accumulation of minor problems can bring great frustration. I don't like to wait in lines. I detest driving in bumper-to-bumper traffic.

Yet I have learned and continue to learn that the petty nuisances of everyday living are precisely God's tools for accomplishing his greatest objective—to conform me to the image of Jesus Christ. That goal was Paul's crown jewel in the cathedral of Romans 8: "For those God foreknew he also predestined to be conformed to the likeness of his Son, that he might be the firstborn among many brothers" (Rom. 8:29).

We actually have the opportunity in this life to be "transformed into his likeness with ever-increasing glory, which comes from the Lord, who is the Spirit" (2 Cor. 3:18). Everything, even the minor irritations, has the potential to be God's instrument for making us like Jesus, to make his will ours, to have his perspective on people and issues.

A visual illustration that helps me understand this principle is my photographic darkroom. When I bring film into the darkroom, the photographic image is already complete. But before it becomes a print, it must go through a harsh developing procedure.

We are complete in Christ. He is in us and we are in him. When we received Christ as Savior, we received his fullness. However, each incident in life, especially the irritations, is a divine developing process that progressively makes us more like him.

What a difference it makes when I keep this big picture in mind. The minor irritations can draw me closer to Christ, making me depend on him in the smallest of details. Because of

this, I can actually give thanks for the irritations. This, of course, as Paul said, comes from the Lord, for I am not capable in my own personality of handling such things with a smile.

What are the little things that annoy you? If you are like me, you have a large list. What happens if you view them as God's tools to allow the life of Christ to be expressed through you? That changes your view doesn't it?

Only in this manner does irritation become inspiration. Like the grain of sand that lodges in an oyster shell and becomes a lovely pearl, the little irritations of life can bring the beauty of Christ's splendor to your inner self.

I don't especially like irritating problems or people, Lord, but I do see the big picture. You have designed everything to help me be like you. That brings meaning to the multitude of aggravations I constantly face. Thank you for the peace this knowledge brings. May Christ's life become mine as I look to him in every detail.

TOUCHSTONE

Understanding God's big picture can turn irritations into inspirations.

In all this, Job did not sin by charging God with wrongdoing.
Job 1:22

The Power of Acceptance

When things go wrong, how do you respond? When your prayers are not answered as you envisioned, how do you act? When a problem appears permanent, what is your reaction?

Do you blame others? Do you withdraw? Do you seek an unacceptable behavioral or emotional method of escape? Perhaps we have all tried some of these tactics and discovered their ultimate futility.

The key to knowing God's peace in such instances is acceptance. By acceptance, I do not mean resignation or passivity. I am not talking about developing a martyr complex or nursing self-pity. What I do mean is taking everything as filtered through the benevolent will of God and trusting him for the results, no matter what that may mean.

This is biblical acceptance in the purest sense. Paul questioned God about his thorn in the flesh, even beseeched him to remove it. But God answered, "My grace is sufficient," and Paul came to terms with his weakness. Jesus prayed passionately in the garden before the Cross but obediently submitted his will to the will of the Father. The prophet Habakkuk wondered why God would use the wicked warriors of Babylon as his rod of correction for the Hebrews. Habakkuk's conclusion was that even if the worst happened, he would still rejoice and trust in God (Hab. 3:17–19). Job queried God repeatedly concerning his calamities but ultimately was forced to acknowledge the sovereignty and power of God and his own inability to understand all of God's ways (Job 42:1–6).

Acceptance enables us to deal with life as it really is, not as we dreamed or hoped it would be. It is a crash course in

authentic faith, enabling us to put our confidence in God when our questions go unanswered, our problems unresolved, our hopes delayed.

It then enables us to go on, and we can wake up each day with the knowledge that we have put ourselves and our situation squarely in the loving hands of our tender heavenly Father. Nothing may change externally, but we change drastically in our spirit and soul. We can cease depleting our spiritual energy on those things we cannot change by leaving them with God and then work positively toward those things we can change with God's gracious help.

> *When I fight against my problems, Lord, I have difficulty resting in your peace. I realize now I can accept my conditions, trusting that you are faithfully at work in my life. I will press on to know you, not striving but simply seeking to be fully submitted to you.*

TOUCHSTONE

In acceptance there is peace.

For our struggle is not against flesh and blood but against the rulers, against the authorities, against the powers of this dark world and against the spiritual forces of evil in the heavenly realms.

Ephesians 6:12

Dressed for the Battle

The peace of God in the life of the believer does not come cheaply or easily, for we have an adversary, the Devil, who is opposed to our spiritual well-being. We can count on the fact that he is subtly, craftily, and nastily at work to steal our contentment and create confusion and discord. Therefore, we must be alert to his tactics and knowledgeable of our defense against his evil schemes.

Each morning I mentally rehearse the list of spiritual pieces of armor that God provides the believer in Ephesians 6:12–18. I verbally put on each piece as my God-given protection against Satan. I begin with the "belt of truth"—the whole counsel of God, the body of Scriptures—as the foundation for my faith. Satan's primary weapon is the lie. Our most potent weapon is the truth. It defeats him every time. Next, I arm myself with the "breastplate of righteousness." That means I am as holy and acceptable in God's eyes as I will ever be. My sins are forgiven, and Satan has no ground for accusation.

I ready myself with the "gospel of peace." I am an ambassador of God's peace wherever I go. I should be prepared to share Christ, sensitive to the opportunities to bring God's peace to men and women who are alienated from him. Then I purposely take up the "shield of faith," which means I choose to live by faith, not by feelings. I will do what God says regardless of the fickleness of my emotions. Then I put on the "helmet of salvation." That is the challenge to renew my mind according to the truth and the security of knowing I have been delivered from the dominion of sin and Satan into God's kingdom. I am not a slave of sin but a child of God. At that point, I am conscious that I can defeat Satan at every turn with the "sword of the Spirit, which is the word of God." This weapon is particular Scriptures that I can use against the enemy as Jesus did when

Satan tempted him. Find a specific Scripture verse for your situation, memorize it, and use it boldly against the adversary.

You will be amazed at the results when you dress for the battle on a daily basis. Satan's attacks will be foiled, his dark schemes exposed, and his tactics thwarted. Satan was conquered at the Cross by Christ (Col. 2:15), and you can experience the power of his conquest and prevailing peace as you put on the armor designed by God.

Christ Jesus, in you I am a victor over all the power of the enemy. May I learn to put on your triumphant armor each day and enjoy your conquest.

TOUCHSTONE

*Be spiritually well dressed
by putting on the whole
armor of God.*

Come to me, all you who are weary and burdened, and I will give you rest. . . . For my yoke is easy and my burden is light.
Matthew 11:28, 30

Our Burden Bearer

Rarely does a day pass when I don't hear the subject of stress discussed. The topic may be something like "burnout" or "chronic fatigue." But the real issue is stress, the pressures of daily life that place us in a weary and parched state of soul and mind.

J. Hudson Taylor, founder of the China Inland Mission, understood such pressures. He lived for years in a strange world with foreign customs. The cultural barriers of sharing the gospel were great. There was the great burden of administering a mission agency and the numerous personnel issues that had to be constantly addressed.

Hanging on the wall of my study is a quote from this godly man that has helped me personally deal with the stress that is generated from pastoring a large church and tending to all of the accompanying duties. It reads: "It doesn't matter, really, how great the pressure is. It only matters where the pressure lies. See that it never comes between you and the Lord—then the greater the pressure, the more it presses you to his breast."

Here is the answer to stress, regardless of its origin, nature, or intensity: Let the pressure drive you to the Source of all your strength, peace, and stability—the Person of Jesus Christ. The apostle Paul came to that wise conclusion after considering the many hardships he endured: "But this happened, that we might not rely on ourselves but on God" (2 Cor. 1:9).

Jesus wants to be our burden bearer. He invites us to come to him with all of our pressures and lay them before him. He asks us to submit to his lordship and realize that once we are yoked together with him, he will uphold us. Coming to Jesus in childlike dependence releases the pressure of our burdens. It lightens the load and enables us to go on. Instead of crumbling and fainting, we find new energy, energy that God himself gives

us as we are driven to him.

A method that a friend once shared with me is particularly helpful in laying our burdens down. Lift your hands up to the Lord. In prayer talk to him about your pressures. When you finish, put your hands down. The physical relief is an immediate reminder that you have done business with God and left your burdens with him.

Let your stress press you to Christ. He will never put on you more than you can bear, for he stands with you to shoulder every load. Once you come to Christ and release your burden to him, there is nothing between you and him but sweet peace. His yoke is light and easy and will not pull you down but lift you up in your time of need.

I am so grateful, Father, that you actually invite me to bring my stress points to you. I need relief from these burdens, and that is what you promise as I cast my pressures on you and submit to your clear and peaceful leadership. Thank you for being my burden bearer for sin and the problems of everyday life.

TOUCHSTONE

Give your burdens to Christ.
He has no load limit.

Oh, how I love your law! I meditate on it all day long.

Psalm 119:97

A Threefold Cord

Peace and quiet. They go together, don't they? That is why consistent quiet times alone with God are so indispensable to experiencing the abiding peace of Christ. Yet I must confess that these times of fellowship with the Lord are occasionally dry and uneventful. Out of a desire to see God work more effectively and personally in my life has come a discovery that has enlivened my quiet times and made them more rewarding than ever.

I begin my quiet time with the reading of Scripture. There really is no other way to know God than through the revelation of his Word by the illumination of the Holy Spirit. If Scripture is not the centerpiece of your quiet time, then it will not impart the supernatural life that every word of God contains. After reading (usually one chapter in a book of the Old Testament and another chapter in the New Testament), I pray. God has answered many, many of my prayers. I have come to know Christ intimately. Yet I thirst for something more—something deeper.

I have come to realize that my thirst is quenched as I spend time meditating on the Word of God. Meditation is not mystical. Rather, it is the extremely practical and nourishing exercise of pondering and thinking on what God is saying through his Word. It is the art of asking questions of the Scriptures and then of yourself and discovering how the truth examined can be applied to your life and the particular problems you face.

Until I gave my quiet time the added dimension of meditation, I never received its rich fullness. Here is how I spend such seasons with the Lord. First, I read the Scriptures. Then I meditate on those portions or verses that God seems to highlight as I read. I may turn and look at other Scriptures that address the same subject. But chiefly, I think carefully and soberly about

what the passage says about God and about my response. This takes time. But it is the best investment of time I know.

Then, after reading and meditating on the Scriptures, I turn to the Lord in prayer. I am amazed at how much I have to pray about. My time of meditation is like a greenhouse for prayer. Prayer becomes a sweet release. It is purposeful and directly connected to what God is saying to me through his Word.

If I read but don't meditate, my prayer life is shallow. If I read and meditate but don't pray, I don't have the pleasure of talking with my Savior and the joy of seeing my specific requests answered. Read. Meditate. Pray. This is the threefold cord that will make your quiet times with Christ more productive and powerful than you can imagine. And the peace of God that comes from personal encounters with him will abound.

Lord, help me to be still and know that you are God. Settle me down so that when I read your Word, I can spend time poring over its rich meaning, meditating on its truth, and seeking to apply it to my circumstances. I trust that my quiet times with you will become even more special and bring me great peace.

TOUCHSTONE

Meditate on God's Word regularly. It is still waters and green pastures to your soul.

Blessed are the peacemakers, for they will be called the sons of God.

Matthew 5:9

The Hard Work
of Peace

K eeping the peace is hard work.
That is why Paul told the Romans to "make every effort to do what leads to peace" (Rom. 14:19). That is why the author of Hebrews said we ought to "make every effort to live in peace with all men" (Heb. 12:14).

God knows that maintaining relational peace with others is not possible without the diligent, conscious exertion of our will and the restraining of our emotions. At no time, however, are we more like Christ than when we are ambassadors of peace, for it is the peacemakers who are called the "sons of God."

A peacemaker is one who is first concerned about pleasing God, not men. When your motivation is to please men, you are caught in relational snarls that can be almost impossible to untie. Your actions are dictated by circumstances and the personalities of individuals. That is an emotional roller coaster where peace is seldom maintained. But when your desire is always to please God, peace with others is far more likely because then your desire is to do what is right in God's sight, even if the consequences are not pleasant for you.

A peacemaker is also one who cultivates a servant's heart. A servant of Jesus Christ is one who not only acknowledges Christ as Lord but also relinquishes to Christ his personal rights. He is keenly interested in the welfare of other believers and will do what is necessary to promote harmony. That may include some difficult moments of self-denial, such as refusing to voice his opinion or declining to defend himself.

A peacemaker is also one who recognizes the danger of a judgmental or critical spirit and commits himself to the edification of the brethren. When wronged, he does not gossip or pass judgment. Jesus said, "Do not judge or you too will be judged" (Matt. 7:1). The peacemaker leaves final judgment and vindication to the Father, who will ultimately bring all truth to light. David knew that God would make his "righteousness shine like the dawn, the justice of [his] cause like the noonday sun" (Ps. 37:6).

Trusting all judgment to Christ without vested self-interest and consumed with the heart of a willing, humble servant, the believer in Christ is free to become a blessed peacemaker in a world of conflict and hostility. He has entrusted his reputation and reward to Christ himself and becomes his ambassador of reconciliation.

It is very difficult, Father, to be a peacemaker. I want to defend myself when conflict arises. Help me to see that you never defended yourself. You did not need to because you were absolutely sure of who you were. I am secure in you. You are the defense of my life. I can bring your peace to others as I confidently rest in my new identity as a new creature in Christ. Make me a peacemaker in my home, my office, my church, wherever I go. I thank you for the blessings you will bring.

TOUCHSTONE

If you desire peace,
  do the things that make
  for peace.

No discipline seems pleasant at the time, but painful. Later on, however, it produces a harvest of righteousness and peace.

Hebrews 12:11

A Harvest of Peace

The most important truth I have learned as a Christian is that Christ is my life. I am an exhibition of his power, an expression of his grace, and an extension of his life.

However, I did not learn that lesson sitting in my study one day. It lodged in my soul during a very difficult time in my life. After many years of ministry, I reached a point of exhaustion. I was not tired of serving God—I was just tired. I lay in bed for about a week and had to rest physically for several months after that. I could not preach. I could not visit the sick. I could not do any of the things I had been accustomed to doing during my ministry.

It was a painful time, but it was the only way God could get my attention for the most magnificent truth I could learn concerning the Christian life—Christ lives in me so that he may live his life through me. At salvation a great exchange took place—my sin for his righteousness, my sin nature for his holy nature. Since that discovery, my preaching, teaching, and daily living have all been founded on the truth that Christ is my life and that he is sufficient for any task.

You may be passing through a rough season right now. Your finances may be low. Your marriage may be strained. There could be any number of circumstances that could be perplexing you. I want you to consider this possibility: Is your current condition the result of God's disciplining hand? God's discipline is not punishment. It is not judgment. It is not an outpouring of his anger. All of that was put on his Son at Calvary. Rather, his discipline is an expression of his love. It is the love of the heavenly Father who seeks to correct and edify us, not condemn us. God's discipline should actually encourage us because it reminds us that we are his beloved children who matter to him so much that he engages in personal correction.

It was the loving discipline of God that put me out of commission for several months so that I could learn the most important lesson of my life, and I am eternally grateful for that. God knows precisely how to get your attention as well for corrective purposes in your life, and that usually involves unpleasant or uncomfortable conditions.

However, notice that the end result of God's discipline is a "harvest of peace and righteousness." Once corrected, we have exciting new fellowship with Christ that is characterized by a wellspring of peace. Obedience is a delight, not a duty. God's ways are not our ways; but when he disciplines us, it is always in love and for our spiritual benefit. Ask God what he is trying to teach you. Accept his correction, learn his truth, and the truth will set you free.

Lord, I realize that I do not especially like discipline. But when you correct me, you always have a goal in mind—that I may share in your holiness and partake yet more of your divine nature that you gave me at salvation. Help me to discern the times when it is your corrective hand at work and let me quickly learn the liberating truth you yearn for me to know.

TOUCHSTONE

*The vinedresser prunes only
for a fruitful harvest.*

I can do everything through him who gives me strength.
Philippians 4:13

Peace Through Strength

I was about forty years old at the time. Miss Bertha Smith was more than seventy years old. Meeting her at the airport one evening, I was amazed at her vitality and enthusiasm.

"Miss Bertha," I asked, "why do you always seem to be three steps ahead of me?" I will never forget the reply of this great missionary: "I don't go in my own strength, Charles. I go in the strength of the Lord. If I had been going in my strength, I would have come home from China years ago."

Miss Bertha certainly knew what she was talking about. Although she lived to be ninety-nine years old, the strength she described wasn't physical but spiritual. It was the same type of supernatural energy Paul referred to in his letter to the Philippian church (Phil. 4:13). Was this some sort of idle boast? Was Paul overstating the case? No, he was simply saying that God would enable him to do whatever he had called him to do. That principle has not changed. When we are weak, he is strong. When we are distraught, he is perfectly calm.

God's strength and the peace that follows in its steps begin when we realize our position in Christ. We are "in Christ," a place where the all-sufficiency of the Savior is completely accessible. God is not distant but resident within. All that he is and has is ours because of our personal relationship with him and the presence of the Holy Spirit. "Through him" we can do all things he calls us to do.

It continues with the right perspective on Christ. He is the Creator, Sustainer, and End of all things. He is the Alpha and the Omega. All power and authority is in Christ. Nothing can withstand his might. This is the Christ who lives in us. We must never diminish the truth that the fullness of deity lives in Christ and we have been given his fullness (Col. 2:9). We do not have to deal with daily problems in human energy but in the resurrection power of Christ.

The question is: Do we tap into this divine fountainhead of God's awesome strength that transforms doubt to confidence, weariness to vigor, and the pessimistic "I can't" to the bold "I can"?

Again, I learned the simple answer from Miss Bertha. She explained, "When I feel burdened and spent, I just pause and remind him of what he promised me and that I am, at this moment, drawing from his resource exactly what I need."

Miss Bertha, Paul, you, and I draw in the same way—by faith. We lean on the promises of God and expect him to do what he says he will do. "Lord Jesus," we say, "I am trusting you for your energy. And I now thank you for it."

In this manner, you can go from strength to strength and find peace that never fails.

I do need to go in your strength, heavenly Father. I am so glad that you give me your strength. I do not have to beg or plead for it but receive it by faith. I give thanks for your strength that sustains me and praise you for empowering me whenever I call on your name.

TOUCHSTONE

God is waiting for you this very moment to call due and payable the promises he has made.

He does not treat us as our sins deserve or repay us according to our iniquities.

Psalm 103:10

Don't Look Back

A former mediocre baseball player raised his batting average almost one hundred points more than the prior season and was named Most Valuable Player in the National League. Asked to explain his dramatic improvement, he said he had learned to focus on the moment at hand. "I don't think about my past at-bats any more," he explained. "I put my failures behind me and concentrate on the present."

Past failures and sins often become the parasitic thief that robs many Christians of God's peace and joy. Somehow such Christians never quite step into the abundant life God has planned for them. They always seem on the verge of stepping into it but are apparently unable to conquer the plague of past mistakes.

The Scriptures are clear on this point: the believer in Jesus Christ is not a victim of his past. He is more than a conqueror through Christ and has the capacity to enjoy each day to its fullest and reach the maximum of his potential for God's kingdom work.

The answer is to understand, embrace, and appropriate by faith each day the radical cure of the Cross—complete forgiveness of sin through Christ's sacrificial death. When Christ died, the guilt and penalty of your sin was placed on him. When you receive him as Savior, you do not have to fear death anymore because Christ died for you. But here is the other part of the good news: You do not have to stagnate in the polluted pool of guilt either, for Jesus was your guilt offering. You can now "draw near to God with a sincere heart in full assurance of faith, having [your] hearts sprinkled to cleanse [you] from a guilty conscience" (Heb. 10:22). God does not condemn you anymore. Why should you condemn yourself? Yes, there may be consequences to your sin that you must still endure, but your

guilt has been taken away. The love and favor of God will help you successfully deal with the aftershocks of sin.

The psalmist said that God has taken away your sin as far as east is from west (Ps. 103:12). That was David's graphic description of God's forgiveness, and he certainly knew the pain of past failures. But his even greater awareness of God's total pardon kept him from belaboring his past defeats and allowed him to become a man after God's own heart.

Is the past stealing today's peace in your life? It doesn't have to anymore. Christ offers you free, full forgiveness so that you may walk in the beauty of his love today and every day. Humble yourself, confess any sin the Holy Spirit convicts you of, receive your pardon in Christ, and concentrate on today's opportunities. You can rise from spiritual mediocrity to a new level of sustained joy and peace in the Lord.

Lord, I see now that what I did wrong ten years ago, ten days ago, or ten minutes ago has already been forgiven through Christ's death on the cross. What freedom there is knowing that I am totally forgiven! There is nothing to match it. Teach me to hate sin as you do so that I may understand the incredible depth of your forgiveness. Thank you for removing the chains of guilt and freeing me to face today's challenges with fresh confidence.

TOUCHSTONE

You cannot move forward looking in the rear-view mirror.

May the God of hope fill you with all joy and peace as you trust in him, so that you may overflow with hope by the power of the Holy Spirit.

Romans 15:13

Regaining Hope

When you have hope for tomorrow, you have the power and peace you need to encounter today's unique set of problems and opportunities. The person who loses hope loses confidence for today and vision for tomorrow. Biblical hope is not fond wishing, it is firm assurance of supernatural help.

Have you reached the point where you are close to giving up hope? Are you so discouraged that the black fog of hopelessness has settled on your soul? That is exactly the place the prophet Jeremiah had reached as he contemplated the destruction of Jerusalem and the temple by the Babylonians.

At the peak of his misery, he inserted this divine ray of hope every believer can cling to in times of despair: "Yet this I call to mind and therefore I have hope: Because of God's great love we are not consumed, for his compassions never fail. They are new every morning; great is your faithfulness. . . . The LORD is good to those whose hope is in him, to the one who seeks him" (Lam. 3:21–23, 25).

When all seems hopeless, hope can be restored as we think about God. It is hard to think about God when our emotions are raw and our confidence is running on vapors, but it is the first step to regaining hope. Deliberately turning your thoughts to God primes the recovery process for hope.

Jeremiah remembered God's great love and compassion. The Hebrew word used for love speaks of the loyal, steadfast, covenant love that God had for his people. God never abandoned them despite sending them seasons of stern discipline. It is that kind of unceasing love that God has for you as his child. It never wanes, it never fails, it never falters. It is not a stale love that lives on past experiences but a daily, renewing, refreshing love that sweeps over your soul moment by moment, day by day. His love is the promise of his provision. Therefore you can

have hope. The love of God for you means that God is now on your side and will stop at nothing to restore your hope in him.

Next, Jeremiah revives his sagging spirit by pondering God's faithfulness. God is faithful to his Word. He will finish what he starts. He is completely trustworthy in every situation and for every unexpected turn of events. Jeremiah also meditates on the goodness of God and the blessings that come from waiting expectantly for him.

The covenant love of God. The unchanging faithfulness of God. The fantastic goodness of God. Think on these things and hope will bear wings that can carry you through every desperate need.

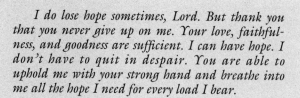

I do lose hope sometimes, Lord. But thank you that you never give up on me. Your love, faithfulness, and goodness are sufficient. I can have hope. I don't have to quit in despair. You are able to uphold me with your strong hand and breathe into me all the hope I need for every load I bear.

TOUCHSTONE

*Hope in God is the staircase
out of despair.*

Cast all your anxiety on him because he cares for you.

1 Peter 5:7

Don't Worry, Be Prayerful

When your automobile comes to a stop sign, the intent of the law is for you to come to a complete halt. Disobeying this injunction can result in disaster for you and others.

It was this kind of authoritative force that Paul used when he told the Philippian believers and us, "Do not be anxious about anything . . ." (Phil. 4:6). The original Greek statement is in the imperative tense, calling for the abrupt stoppage of an action. The rich fullness of the Greek can be read in this way: Stop perpetually worrying about even one very little thing. What an amazing command! God is actually forbidding us to worry or fret about anything. Of course, there are normal concerns, but that is not what the Bible is talking about. It is addressing the distracting, anxious cares that gnaw at our soul, allowing little or no room for God's peace to abide. "Just stop it and don't do it anymore," Paul commands.

Easy to say, hard to do. Right? Well, the doing of it is both hard and easy. Hard in the sense that God's Word often asks us to behave in ways contrary to our natural conduct. But it is also easy once we understand that God never asks us to do something for which he does not enable and equip us. Paul's divine prescription against worry is found in the remainder of Philippians 4:6: ". . . but in everything, by prayer and petition, with thanksgiving, present your requests to God."

Paul says in essence that we should worry about nothing by praying about everything. Paul is not referring to a lethargic, generic kind of praying but vigorous, concentrated prayer of the highest sort. The word for prayer suggests the thought and activity of worship and devotion. It is coming to God and rec-

ognizing his power, wisdom, and presence. It is the kind of praying that basks in the greatness of God, exalting his ability to handle all of our worries in his sovereign wisdom.

The use of the word *petition* refers to our specific requests. This is a critical step if we are to truly experience freedom from worry. We first worship God and then present to him our very detailed situation that is causing us to fret. In effect, we are transferring our worrisome circumstance into the capable hands of Almighty God. We are plain, blunt, and to the point in our requests. We don't mince words. We tell God what is bothering us. Then we move into thanksgiving, grateful that our awesome God has heard our requests and will answer us according to his goodness and graciousness. We need not worry. God himself takes on our problems, and his peace replaces our apprehension. Worry is nothing but unbelief. Trusting God with our anxieties through reverent and definitive prayer is the way to stop worry in its destructive tracks and move through our day with the serenity that only God can give.

When I worry, I find it hard to pray. I realize now that prayer is exactly what I need to do in such times. Help me not to wander when I pray but to bring the very thing that troubles me to your attention. Then help me to trust in your ability to handle my worries.

've
TOUCHSTONE

*Worry about nothing by
praying about everything.*

So David and his men wept aloud until they had no strength left to weep. . . . But David found strength in the LORD his God.
1 Samuel 30:4, 6

From Pity Party to Praise

A pity party is nothing to celebrate, but we have to admit we all have our share of them. They are unproductive, self-defeating, and faith-deflating; and they create a spiritual atmosphere that numbs us to the peace of God.

When David and his warriors returned to their home in Ziklag, they discovered it ravaged and burned. Its inhabitants, including David's family, had been taken captive by the invading Amalekite army. The time was never more ripe for a grand pity party for the former shepherd boy. David's leadership was in question. He had been on the run from Saul for years and fled for shelter among the Philistines, Israel's traditional enemy. David's own soldiers were primed for mutiny and talked of stoning him. David wept. David mourned. David cried. But he turned his pity party around by finding "strength in the Lord his God." While there are no Scriptures that tell how David escaped the suffocating coils of self-pity, I think he must have thought on several things.

I believe David must have reviewed his past. He thought about how God had worked in his life, keeping him from the many schemes and traps of Saul. David probably reflected upon the Lord, considering the intimacy of his personal relationship with Jehovah God and God's faithfulness through the years. Then I imagine that David must have remembered the promises of the God who had taken him from the sheepfold and declared his intent to establish David as king of Israel.

I think David then found strength to go to God in prayer, making a request for God's guidance. We know that David "inquired of the Lord" (1 Sam. 30:8) regarding the pursuit of

the raiding party and found God's specific direction. David gave chase, discovered the camp of the enemy, defeated them, and recovered his family and goods.

What God did for David he will do for you. You do not have to wallow in the mire of self-pity any longer. You can choose to allow God to pull you out of the pit as you review God's past blessings, reflect on the majesty and might of God, remember the promises of God that apply to your particular situation (if you are fearful, find verses on fear; if you feel depressed, search out verses on God's comfort and presence), and then make big requests of God for future guidance and protection.

The pity party will end. Praise will magnify the presence and power of God. You will find victory where there has been defeat, and perfect peace where there has been agony of soul. The choice is yours.

Forgive me for feeling sorry for myself, Lord. That is a dead-end street. Change my perspective so that I may sense your presence and care. Lift me out of the pit and put a new song in my mouth, a song of praise to you.

TOUCHSTONE

*When you are in the pit,
God is at his pinnacle.*

I have learned the secret of being content in any and every situation.

Philippians 4:12

The Key to Contentment

One of my favorite spiritual disciplines is reading a chapter of Proverbs each day. A particular passage that has consistently helped me maintain a spiritual equilibrium of contentment and peace is Proverbs 30:8–9: "Give me neither poverty nor riches, but give me only my daily bread. Otherwise, I may have too much and disown you and say, 'Who is the LORD?' Or I may become poor and steal, and so dishonor the name of my God."

Like many, I struggle with the issue of contentment. How much is enough? Should I be satisfied with what I have or seek more? Is ambition wrong? What kind of goals should I have? The answers are not easy, but I believe God's Word provides the balance we need to cultivate godly contentment in our spiritual development and physical needs.

I need to begin with the basics. The most important is a vital, growing relationship with Jesus Christ. That is the foundation for contentment. Only when my chief delight is in Jesus Christ am I able to put into perspective the peripheral issues of material goods and personal ambition. Paul wrote to Timothy, "Godliness with contentment is great gain. For we brought nothing into the world, and we can take nothing out of it. But if we have food and clothing, we will be content with that" (1 Tim. 6:6–8). Concentrate on knowing God and realize that material objects are important only so far as your stewardship is concerned.

That happens as we refuse to be conformed to "the pattern of this world" and become "transformed by the renewing of [our] mind" (Rom. 12:2). The lust of the eyes and the lust of the flesh always want more. They are fast tracks for the allure of deceit and manipulation of a world system riddled with greed and craving. Renewing our mind means we program them with the principles of Scripture. We make decisions based on the truth of God's Word. That keeps us on an even keel when the pull of the world tugs disproportionately at our pocketbooks or hearts.

We must learn to live on a daily basis. Jesus told us to pray for our "daily bread"—the sufficient provision for today's necessities. Contentment most often is lost when we worry about the future. God is in control of that, and we must leave tomorrow's problems with him. Today I can bring my needs to Christ. Today his grace is sufficient. Jesus "daily bears our burdens" (Ps. 68:19).

Above all, the key to contentment is learning that I can do everything God wants me to do through his enablement. I can set faith-building goals that are in God's will. Ambition is okay so long as my chief objective is to glorify Christ, not myself. God does not want us to do everything, but he will help us do what he has planned for our lives. We can be content knowing that he empowers us to deal with all the ups and downs of life as we wholeheartedly depend on him.

Contentment is a daily battle. It is something we learn by sticking to the basics—nurturing a growing relationship with Jesus Christ, living one day at a time, and knowing that Christ in us strengthens us for every challenge. This is great gain and gives great peace.

Contentment is hard to learn. But I know, Lord, that you can give me peace in every circumstance and the contentment it brings as I submit to your lordship. Teach me to trust you for each day's problems and rely on you to strengthen me for every task. I can be content as long as I know you are with me, helping me at every turn.

TOUCHSTONE

*A contented heart is one
that allows Christ to set
the agenda.*

*See to it that no one misses the grace of God and that no bitter
root grows up to cause trouble and defile many.*

Hebrews 12:15

Rooting Out Bitterness

O ne of the greatest barriers that prevents us from experiencing God's unsurpassed peace is a root of bitterness. Planted as a seed of anger, rejection, or resentment, bitterness grows into a poisonous emotion that chokes out the peace of God in our lives and defiles the lives of family members and friends.

If you are or have been embittered against someone because of an unjust circumstance, you know the emotional price you pay. It affects you physically and spiritually, releasing its hostile toxins at the slightest upset. You cannot hide a bitter spirit. It spills over into all that you do.

But the good news of the gospel is freedom from every form of bondage, including a bitter spirit. You do not have to be its slave or allow it to fester a day longer. In honest prayer before God, admit your bitterness. Be specific. Acknowledge it as sin and repent, changing your mind and heart about its corrosive influence. This attacks the problem at its root—sin against God—and creates the right climate for healing and restoration.

Next comes one of the most difficult steps toward dislodging the stronghold of bitterness. You must choose to view the offending party or circumstance as God's tool in your life. That is fundamental to long-term freedom. Everything that comes into your life is filtered through the will of God. God has allowed this person or event, as painful as it may be, to touch your life for your personal spiritual growth. This is the extraordinary biblical view that will excavate the root of bitterness from your spirit. You are not a victim of injustice or vengeance but a child of God who can respond to every circumstance in the light of the fact that he is in control and he has allowed it for his good purpose.

Accepting that truth allows you to move on to extending grace and forgiveness. You did not deserve God's grace. Others do not deserve his grace. But he freely extends it to you regardless of your performance. You are called to freely extend it to others who hurt you as well. There is no limit to forgiveness or grace. When you forgive another person, choosing to treat others as Christ treats you, then you are replacing the cancer of bitterness with the superabundant, healing love of God. "Be kind and compassionate to one another, forgiving each other, just as in Christ God forgave you" (Eph. 4:32).

Bitterness causes us to come short of God's grace, not to fall from it. Let the grace of God do its work in your heart, and bitterness will have no room to sprout and spread.

Dear Lord, when you hung on the cross, you had no bitterness toward your persecutors because you knew they were tools in your Father's hand to accomplish the marvelous work of redemption through your death, burial, and resurrection. May I see those who offend me in this same divine light and so be rescued and delivered from the venom of a bitter spirit. Thank you for your grace and forgiveness that make healing possible.

TOUCHSTONE

Bitterness can find no root
in the rich soil of grace.

Be transformed by the renewing of your mind. Then you will be able to test and approve what God's will is—his good, pleasing and perfect will.

Romans 12:2

Peace and Good Will

When I came to First Baptist Church of Atlanta more than twenty years ago, I encountered much opposition. One truth sustained and kept me through the many conflicts: I knew I had obeyed the will of God. He had put me there. I could accept the challenges with complete confidence.

There is little peace for the person who consistently follows his own instincts instead of seeking God's plan. But the person who knows he is in step with Christ can experience steady peace even in tight places. When Paul and Silas were called by God to preach in Macedonia, they quickly found themselves in a prison cell. But they sang praises instead of grumbling, because they knew they had followed God obediently and wholeheartedly.

"But if God would just send angels and tell me where to go and what to do, I could sing praise psalms as well," you say. I understand. I feel that way sometimes too. But what I have realized is that God has given me the full revelation of his Word to impart wisdom and counsel sufficient for every demand. He has not left me to grope in the dark. The light of his Word is available for my decision making, and the Holy Spirit lives in me to make it clear.

The key is to be principle-centered. A Bible principle is an eternal truth with universal application. For instance, we reap what we sow. If you hang around bad friends, trouble is not far away. God may not tell me which house to buy or which car to drive, but his principles of finance provide accurate guidelines. If you stay in the Scriptures, your desire to do God's will eventually intersects with a principle of Scripture. We must do more than pull Bible promises out of the scriptural hat, accept them as God's confirmation, and move on.

Sometimes God will use a certain verse to direct us; but most often, he leads us by aligning our decisions with biblical principles. We must be willing to seek God's will. He invites us to ask him for guidance and wisdom because he cares for us. He wants us to do his will because he desires that we glorify him. It is not that we have to overcome God's hesitance to impart information; we have only to receive humbly and patiently what he gladly gives. Even when we make the wrong decision and reap the unpleasant consequences, we are never outside the love of God. We admit our mistake, confess our sin if we were disobedient, and then trust God to lead us from that point.

We must keep in mind that God is most interested in revealing himself in the decision-making process. He wants us to know him as the Guide rather than merely receiving right guidance from him. He wants to us know him supremely.

You can know and do the will of God. It is not complex. Live in obedience to him, read and study his Word, wait for his answer, and more than likely you will find yourself doing the good, pleasing, and perfect will of God. In his will is a stable, fixed peace.

> *Lord, it is good to know that you desire for me to know your will even more than I desire to know it. I am your servant; and like any servant, I receive my directions from the Master. I understand that it may take time for your will to be grasped, but I thank you for giving me enough truth and light to make daily decisions that move me in your direction. Above all, thank you for drawing me closer to you. And the better I know you, the more likely I will discover your plan.*

TOUCHSTONE

*Seek the Guide, and
guidance is sure
to follow.*

*And the peace of God, which transcends all understanding,
will guard your hearts and your minds in Christ Jesus.*

Philippians 4:7

Peace of Mind

Peace of mind. Everyone is looking for it. Only God can deliver it. It is a peace detached from external factors, above and beyond sheer logic, victorious over raw emotions.

It is the kind of peace every follower of Christ can access. It is not reserved for merely tragic moments, though it certainly is sufficient in such instances. It is available in unlimited portions for everyday living, every decision, every obstacle, every circumstance.

There is, of course, no formula for such peace, for it is tailor-made by the God of peace for each individual, for each situation. There are, however, several pervasive principles of Scripture that are spiritual pathways to this exquisite peace of heart and mind.

Peace that passes understanding is grounded on a spiritual mindset: "The mind controlled by the Spirit is life and peace" (Rom. 8:6). The mind controlled by the Spirit views all of life from God's perspective. It is constantly nourished by the Word of God and is focused on the priority of spiritual principles above the philosophy and mindset of the world. It filters all of our thoughts, emotions, and contemplations through the pure grid of the Scriptures. Our minds are yielded to the Spirit's influence and direction.

Such peace is experienced as we avoid the worrisome tug of double-mindedness. James wrote that the double-minded man is "unstable in all he does" (James 1:8). The believer asks God for wisdom, makes his requests clearly known, and then thanks God for the answer. He is singled-minded in that he expects God to act and refuses to entertain the twin evils of doubt and unbelief.

Transcendent peace is cultivated by thinking on the things that Paul calls "true, noble, right, pure, lovely, admirable, excellent, and praiseworthy" (Phil. 4:8). You are called to have your mind dwell on good things and think cheerfully about the future. Positive thinking is simply allowing your mind to meditate on truth. Your mind is renewed. Your personality is reprogrammed by the powerful, living Word of God to think as he thinks.

When all this is done, you can say along with Paul that "the God of peace will be with you" (Phil. 4:9). Peace of mind inevitably leads to peaceful living. A supernatural quality of contentment and calm rests at the center of your heart, protecting and shielding you from the excessive fretfulness of this world. Chaos may swirl around you, but you are anchored to the unchanging peace of Christ.

The Source of peace gives transcendent peace. It is for you. It is for you today. It is a gift you receive by confident faith. Embrace it, and you will not exchange it for anything the world may offer.

Jesus, I am truly amazed how you give your peace for everyday living. When I am torn apart, your peace calms me as I turn aside from the distractions and allow the Holy Spirit to control my thoughts. Sometimes your peace rushes in. Sometimes it takes awhile. But it does come as I continue to gaze upon you. Be the health of my countenance, O Lord, as you guard my emotions and thoughts with your shield of peace.

TOUCHSTONE

*The Source of peace
gives transcendent
peace to you.*

So we say with confidence, "The Lord is my helper; I will not be afraid. What can man do to me?"

Hebrews 13:6

Preparing for the Future

The most prevalent emotion concerning the future is fear. Since we do not know what tomorrow holds, we lean toward a degree of tension and uncertainty, which breeds timidity and undermines our confidence in God. Of course, certain fears are appropriate. We should be afraid to stick our hands in a snake den or a hot fire. That's only common sense. But there are hordes of unnecessary, unhealthy fears of today and tomorrow that erode our peace and create unsettled spiritual footing for fighting the good fight of faith.

Knowing that God is in control of all things should lessen much of our apprehension. We know that God is with us, so we can obey the many scriptural injunctions that tell us, "Fear not . . ." But often our fears are so stubbornly ingrained that it takes more than a knowledge of God's providence and an awareness of his presence to put fear to flight.

Here is one biblical principle that has helped me deal with my personal fears and I believe will comfort and encourage you too: The more I understand and accept God's amazing love for me, the less I fear life's uncertainties. That was the apostle John's antidote for fear: "There is no fear in love. But perfect love drives out fear. . . . The one who fears is not made perfect in love" (1 John 4:18).

God cares for me with absolutely perfect love. That means he is taking care of all my needs, including my future ones. As I rest in his constant, unceasing love for me, fear is banished. What do I need to be afraid of if God himself is caring for me? Why should the future frighten me if God promises he will provide his all-sufficient love for every situation? Bask in the love of

God. Think on the love of God. Embrace the love of God. When you do, the many concerns and issues that can generate fear will be expelled by the awesome love of God.

If we allow our fear to drive us to a greater appreciation and appropriation of the love of God, then our fears actually lead us to greater trust and dependence on the Father. David said, "When I am afraid, I will trust in you" (Ps. 56:3). God does not give you fear but power, love, and a sound and well-balanced mind (2 Tim. 1:7). As a ship's weight displaces water, the love of God will dislodge all your fears.

Jesus told the crowds, "Do not be afraid, little flock, for your Father has been pleased to give you the kingdom" (Luke 12:32). You are a member of the flock under God's care. He will never leave or forsake you. That truth should melt your fears. It should dissolve your alarm and terror. You are a sheep in God's fold, and God takes perfect care of his flock. The Good Shepherd loves you and provides for you. May every apprehension thaw under the light of God's perfect love for you.

I am not sure I understand how perfect your love for me is, Father, but I do know that it is better than I can possibly imagine. My fears, and I do have several, have no place when I allow your love to govern and guide me. Every trace of terror is gone when I think of being under your watchful care. Thank you for the peace and security that truth brings and help me to apply it daily. When fear arises, may it drive me into your love and so make me more dependent on you and less susceptible to the "what ifs" of life.

TOUCHSTONE

*God knows all of your
"what ifs" and has
provided all of the
"will be's" for them.*

Your promises have been thoroughly tested, and your servant loves them.

Psalm 119:140

An Encouraging
Word

In the margin next to many Scripture verses in my Bible are clearly marked dates. Each one indicates an instance when God spoke to me through the verse to encourage me in times of testing or adversity. I cannot tell you how many times a Bible promise has sustained me in difficult straits. It is light in darkness, strength in weakness, and nourishing manna for my soul.

A Bible promise is God's Word of encouragement for you to claim by faith and cling to in rough waters. When a battered Paul was hesitant to stay in Corinth, God promised him safekeeping (Acts 18:9–10). When the ship that was transferring him to Rome was about to sink, God sent an angel to Paul to declare that he would stand before Caesar and the lives of all those aboard would be spared (Acts 27:23–24). When Joshua prepared to enter the Promised Land, God encouraged him with the assurance of his presence and deliverance from the land's inhabitants (Josh. 1:2–9).

A Bible promise from God is a declaration of his intention to graciously bestow a gift upon his children. Some promises are conditional, fulfilled only upon the believer's obedience to a clearly stated condition. For example, if you want to experience God's best financially, you must first give of your resources. Other promises have specific limitations, such as God's covenant promise to Abraham that he would become the father of many nations. But there are many promises God desires to see claimed and appropriated in our lives that require only trust in him.

God's promises usually meet a specific need in your life. You may be reading the Scriptures, and a verse becomes

divinely highlighted by the Holy Spirit. This is a promise from God you may claim if you do not take it out of context (manipulate it to apply to an irrelevant situation) and if your interpretation of it does not contradict any other portion of Scripture. The Spirit of God witnesses to your spirit that it is from him, and the ultimate purpose is to glorify God.

When God speaks to you in such a way, you have a promise that will anchor your mind, will, and emotion. You can meditate on it day and night, standing on the authority and power of the Word of God. It becomes part of your being.

God's promises have never let me down. God cannot lie. If you will discipline yourself to read his Word consistently and obediently and wait patiently and submissively for him to fulfill his promises, you will discover truth you can stand on in any weather. Nothing promotes peace like God's encouraging Word.

Thank you, Lord, for inviting me to stand on your promises. I know I can count on you. When you speak to me in this way, I am greatly blessed. I have the strength to endure, the hope to continue. Make me sensitive to your Word and bold to claim your promises.

TOUCHSTONE

A Bible promise is God's guaranteed means of encouragement.